Don't Put Your Pants on Your Head, Fred!

Caryl Hart • Leigh Hodgkinson

ORCHARD

"**Don't** put your pants on your head, Fred!
Don't wear six pairs at a time.

Are you **sure** those pink frillies are yours, Fred?
I'm thinking that maybe . . . they're mine . . .

Don't wear those boxers *again*, Fred!
They're crawling around on their own.

Where are your clean ones?
Here, try on these green ones.

Get moving,
or Mum won't
half moan."

Mum tells me to change my pants daily
But I can't decide which ones to choose.
Then Kate says, "Don't worry, just do what I say,
We'll soon sort your pants, clothes and shoes."

"Put on some undies,
There's lots in the drawer.

Make sure they're fresh
And **not** picked off the floor.

Get warm, woolly, blue ones,
So what if they're tight?

One foot in
each leg hole . . .

No no!

That's not right!

Pants go on **first**
Then put trousers on top.
Now do up your buttons –
Don't jiggle. Don't hop.

Your shirt's inside out,
And those socks aren't a pair.
Now, tie up your laces
And **do** comb your hair!"

I slump in my room in confusion.
My clothes are just driving me barmy!
So, I send my best pilot

to ask for support

From the head of

Her

Majesty's

Army.

DeaR
SerGeant SMart,
CAN You hELP
me...

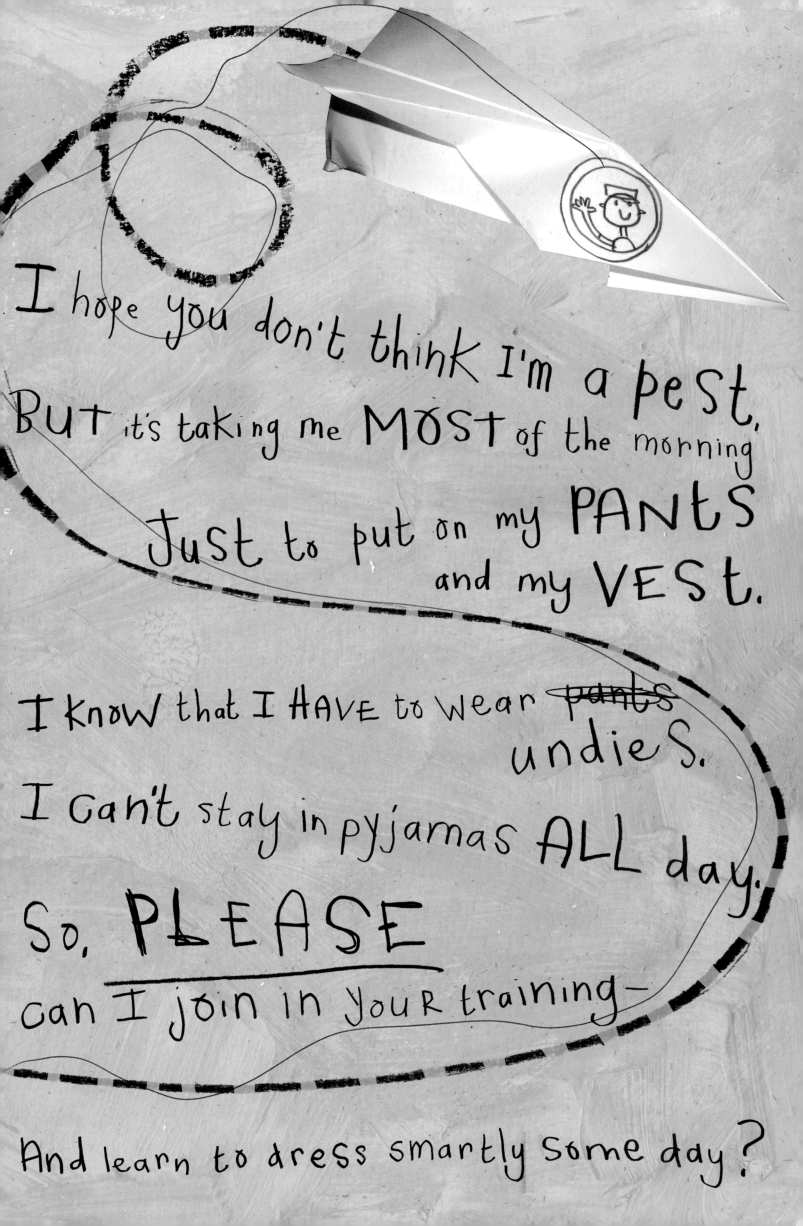

I hope you don't think I'm a pest,
But it's taking me MOST of the morning
Just to put on my PANTS
and my VEST.

I know that I HAVE to wear ~~pants~~ undies.
I can't stay in pyjamas ALL day.
So, PLEASE
can I join in your training—

And learn to dress smartly some day?

The next day there's a ring on the doorbell.

"There's a horse
here to see you,"
yells Kate.

trit trot trit

The horse hands me a note from the Sergeant,
It says, "Come to the fort. Don't be late!"

We **gallop** through gardens and parkland, And *race* through a field full of sheep.

But when we arrive at the fortress,

The soldiers are still

fast asleep!

"Ah, there you are Fred!"
  yawns the Sergeant.
"Come straight up the stairs to our room!
We've got an exciting inspection today,
The Queen says she'll be here at noon."

SOLDIERS'
BEDROOM
(PRIVATE)

DRUMSTICK
ROOM

CAMOUFLAGE
ROOM

MEDAL
ROOM

BOOT
ROOM

DUNGEON

"But it's half-past eleven already!" I cry.

"Aren't you meant to be up, washed and dressed?

Quick, wake up the soldiers! There's no time to lose! You must all look your finest and best!"

"But no one knows how," says the Sergeant,
And he looks round the room in dismay.

SOLDIERS'
BED ROOM
(PRIVATE)

"It only takes **you** half
the morning to dress,
We've been trying
to do it for days!"

"But you're meant to be experts!" I stutter.
"I was hoping that *you* could teach me!
But do what I say, and we should be OK.
Now what did Kate say, let me see . . .

Ah yes . . ."

"Pick up some undies,
There's **lots** on the floor.
They won't **itch** or **scritch**
If you've worn them before?

One arm in each leg hole.
Three pairs at a time.
If you can't find
   your own pants
Then . . .
   wear some of **mine**?

Pyjamas go under . . .
Then pants go on top?
Tie your laces together
It helps you to hop.

hoppity hop hop

Wear your shirt inside out . . .
Put your socks on a pear.
Leave your buttons undone
And then mess up your hair?"

The soldiers rush round in a panic –
They grab all the pants they can find.
They **struggle** and **wiggle**,
they fall over
and **giggle**
Then march out in a wobbly line.

They have pants round their ankles
And pants up their legs.
They have pants on their elbows
And pants on their heads . . .

. . . There are pants on their drumsticks,
And pants on their hats,
And someone has even put
Pants on the cat!

"How's THAT!" beams the Sergeant. "We're ready!"
"Are you sure?" I say. "Something looks weird."
"Ah, yes," says the Sergeant, "Quick, pass me a pen,
I forgot my moustache and my beard!"

"Oh, my word!"

cries the Queen with a giggle.
"That's not how you're
meant to get dressed!

You're supposed to take off your pyjamas,
Then put on clean pants and a vest.

Next, pull on your trousers
and t-shirt.
Or you could wear
a skirt, or a dress.
If it's cold wear a jumper,
a jacket,
or coat,

Then you'll all look
your finest and best!"

So, we quickly get changed in the fortress,
And much to the Sergeant's delight . . .

We pass the inspection!

"Well done!" cheers the Queen.

"This time you have got it
just right!"

We line up and stand to attention,
Then, to show off the effort we've made,
We march out to the sound of the drummers,

On our very own **Royal Pants Parade!**